The [Donkey] Who Was Lost

LUKE 2:41-52 FOR CHILDREN

Written by Alyce Bergey

Illustrated by Betty Wind

ARCH Books

COPYRIGHT © 1972 CONCORDIA PUBLISHING HOUSE, ST. LOUIS, MISSOURI

CONCORDIA PUBLISHING HOUSE LTD., LONDON, E. C. 1

MANUFACTURED IN THE UNITED STATES OF AMERICA

ISBN 0-570-06065-6

Bright flowers bloomed in Nazareth.
Sweet birds sang everywhere.
Soft breezes blew as Jesus combed
the donkey's coat with care.

His friend, Tobias, wandered by.
"Hi, Toby!" Jesus called.
"Passover's here and this year we
can go – we're twelve years old!
We'll see the temple and other things.
Tomorrow is the day
we all start for Jerusalem –
a hundred miles away!"

Next morning early Jesus helped
tie bundles of supplies
upon the little donkey's back,

and then neath sunny skies,
with all the other families,
they started up the road.

Young Jesus proudly led the small
gray donkey with its load.

Clippety-clop! The donkey train
moved slowly on its way.
The people sang and talked as on
they marched.

At last one day –

"Look! I can see Jerusalem!"
cried Jesus in delight.

They soon were there.
The wide-eyed boys
looked round at every sight:

the towers tall, the golden gate,
the city's high stone walls,

the crowds of people
in the streets,
the bright,
gay market stalls.

"Look, Jesus!" Toby said.
"Up there!
The great
white temple! See?"
"Look at the shining
golden roof!"
cried Jesus
happily.

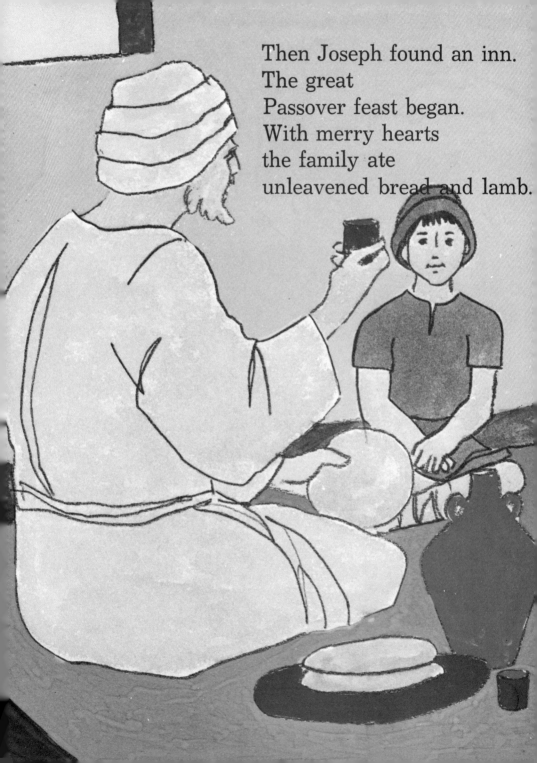

Then Joseph found an inn.
The great
Passover feast began.
With merry hearts
the family ate
unleavened bread and lamb.

"Passover tells us of the night
God set our people free
by His great love," said Joseph. Then
they all sang joyfully.

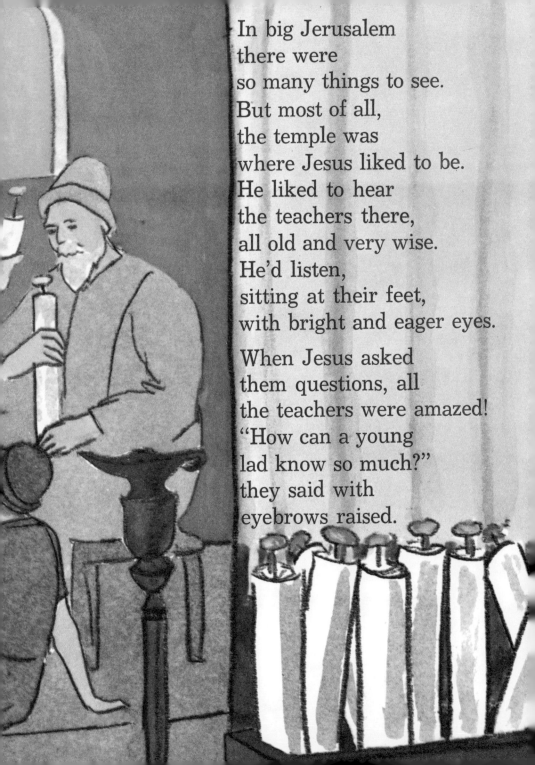

In big Jerusalem
there were
so many things to see.
But most of all,
the temple was
where Jesus liked to be.
He liked to hear
the teachers there,
all old and very wise.
He'd listen,
sitting at their feet,
with bright and eager eyes.

When Jesus asked
them questions, all
the teachers were amazed!
"How can a young
lad know so much?"
they said with
eyebrows raised.

The people stayed a week. And then,
one morning bright and clear,
they started back toward Nazareth.

But as the night drew near,
"Where's Jesus?" Joseph asked his wife.
"I don't know!" she replied.
"He must be with the other boys."

She called His name and cried.
No answer came! They quickly wen
and found the other lads.
"Have you seen Jesus?"
Joseph asked.
Not any of them had!

They looked and looked for Jesus
and soon became quite worried.
"He isn't here!" they cried. Back to
Jerusalem they hurried!

The next day in the city streets
and at each market stall
they both asked: "Tell us, have you seen
a boy – about so tall?"

"His name is Jesus. He's my son.
We lost Him!" Mary said.
But one by one the merchants and
the strangers shook their heads.

They hurried to the inn where they
had stayed when they were there.
They cried, "We can't find Jesus! Have
you seen Him anywhere?"

But NO one had seen Jesus! And
now Mary was alarmed.
"What's happened to my son?" she cried.
"Oh, maybe He's been harmed!"

Three days had passed. Said Joseph then,
"I know where He might be!
He loved God's house. He could be there."
They quickly ran to see.

When they had reached
the temple church,
they were surprised
and glad!
For there among
the teachers sat
just one young,
bright-eyed lad.

Around Him
many people stood,
all listening in surprise.
"Look!" Joseph said.
"It's Jesus with
the teachers
great and wise!"

Then Jesus' mother went to Him.
Her heart was full of joy,
but scolding just a bit, she said,
"We were alarmed, my Boy!

"We looked all over for You, Son.
Oh, why did You stay here?
We thought that You were lost!" she said
and wiped away a tear.

But gently Jesus said to them,
"Why did you look for Me?
Didn't you know My Father's house
is where I'd surely be?"

They didn't understand His words.
But Mary smiled, and then
the three of them went down the road
to Nazareth again.

The Boy obeyed His parents, and
as years passed one by one,
He grew and learned still more.
How pleased God was with His dear Son!

DEAR PARENTS:

In so many ways Jesus was a regular boy as He was growing up in Nazareth. He had all the usual experiences of a happy childhood. Mary and Joseph couldn't have asked for a better child.

But in one respect the boy Jesus was unusual. He was closely tied, in thoughts and ambitions, to His heavenly Father. He enjoyed going to church — as His ancestor David had — and He delighted in His conversations with God.

This became very obvious when He stayed behind in Jerusalem at the age of twelve. Mary and Joseph worried about His absence. But what a desirable kind of worry for parents to suffer!

What parents would not exchange this kind of worry for that which is caused by delinquency and rebellion? The hunger for God's Word in the case of Jesus was fed with the promises of God and with the strength to love.

Parents also can take a lesson from this incident. They can remember that their children are individuals and that as teen-agers they must be readied for responsibility and trust and encouraged to act on their religious convictions.

Have your children tell you — after a visit to church or Sunday school — what they liked the most about their study and worship. If they have negative feelings, let them feel free to express them, and together with them examine how you might together look for values in worship you may have been missing.

And thank God, with relief, for the curiosity your child has about the things of his heavenly Father.

THE EDITOR